Littlest Pet Shop

THE ULTIMATE HANDBOOK

VOLUME 4

By Samantha Brooke

SCHOLASTIC INC.

New York   Toronto   London   Auckland   Sydney
Mexico City   New Delhi   Hong Kong   Buenos Aires

ISBN-13: 978-0-545-06234-3
ISBN-10: 0-545-06234-9

12 11 10 9 8 7 6 5 4 3 2   9 10 11 12 13 14/0

Printed in the U.S.A.
First printing, January 2009

TABLE OF CONTENTS

REAL FEEL

These bobble-headed friends each have something special about them. Some are soft to the touch. Others are scaly, sparkly, or have shining eyes. No matter what makes them special, they're sure to be some of your very favorite pets.

SCOTTIE

EYE COLOR: Sky blue

BODY COLOR: Black

FAVORITE ACCESSORY: Pink tent

LIKES: Camping

DISLIKES: Bug bites

FAVORITE VACATION SPOT: The mountains

MOST LIKELY TO: Go hiking

DRAGONFLY

EYE COLOR: Teal

BODY COLOR: Pink and purple

FAVORITE ACCESSORY: Sparkly wings

LIKES: Drinking nectar

DISLIKES: Walking

FAVORITE VACATION SPOT: In the clouds

MOST LIKELY TO: Fly really fast

CAT

EYE COLOR: Violet

BODY COLOR: Cream and brown

FAVORITE ACCESSORY: Sunblock

LIKES: Playing with birds

DISLIKES: Getting wet

FAVORITE VACATION SPOT: The park

MOST LIKELY TO: Make new friends

GOLDEN RETRIEVER

EYE COLOR: Ice blue

BODY COLOR: Golden

FAVORITE ACCESSORY: Pen and paper

LIKES: Collecting stamps

DISLIKES: Junk mail

FAVORITE VACATION SPOT: Anywhere there are postcards

MOST LIKELY TO: Send you a care package

TURTLE

EYE COLOR: Green

BODY COLOR: Lime green

FAVORITE ACCESSORY: Beach towel

LIKES: Surfing

DISLIKES: Sunburns

FAVORITE VACATION SPOT: The Bahamas

MOST LIKELY TO: Collect seashells

CAT

EYE COLOR: Grass green

BODY COLOR: Charcoal gray

FAVORITE ACCESSORY: A brush and comb

LIKES: Having soft fur

DISLIKES: Tangles

FAVORITE VACATION SPOT: The salon

MOST LIKELY TO: Get a haircut

GECKO

EYE COLOR:
Yellow-green

BODY COLOR: Orange

FAVORITE ACCESSORY:
Orange jacket

LIKES: Hanging up clothes

DISLIKES: Wrinkles

FAVORITE VACATION SPOT:
Fifth Avenue

MOST LIKELY TO:
Buy things on sale

FISH

EYE COLOR: Green and yellow

BODY COLOR:
Blue and yellow

FAVORITE ACCESSORY: Flippers

LIKES: Blowing bubbles

DISLIKES: Warm baths

FAVORITE VACATION SPOT: The Arctic

MOST LIKELY TO: Build a sand castle

PARROT

EYE COLOR: Emerald green

BODY COLOR: Red, orange, blue

FAVORITE ACCESSORY:
Eye patch

LIKES: Finding treasure

DISLIKES: Choppy water

FAVORITE VACATION SPOT:
On a cruise ship

MOST LIKELY TO: Say "Argh!"

SPIDER

EYE COLOR: Olive green

BODY COLOR: Purple

FAVORITE ACCESSORY:
Spiderweb

LIKES: Knitting

DISLIKES: Knots

FAVORITE VACATION SPOT:
Anywhere tropical

MOST LIKELY TO:
Knit you something

CHOW CHOW

EYE COLOR: Light green

BODY COLOR: Golden brown

FAVORITE ACCESSORY:
Pink tiara

LIKES: Being a princess

DISLIKES: Dungeons

FAVORITE VACATION SPOT:
The palace

MOST LIKELY TO: Have a ball

PENGUIN

EYE COLOR: Mint green

BODY COLOR:
Black, white, and yellow

FAVORITE ACCESSORY: Sled

LIKES: Ice cream

DISLIKES: Warm weather

FAVORITE VACATION

SPOT: A ski resort

MOST LIKELY TO: Eat sushi

SQUEAKY CLEAN

These fun-loving pets always like to look their best. Be sure to keep these little friends in tip-top condition so they can really shine!

BIRD

EYE COLOR:
Yellow and green

BODY COLOR: Turquoise

FAVORITE ACCESSORY: Birdbath

LIKES: Getting clean

DISLIKES: Dirt

FAVORITE VACATION SPOT:
A spa

MOST LIKELY TO:
Ask for a facial

MOUSE

EYE COLOR: Lavender

BODY COLOR: Light brown

FAVORITE ACCESSORY:
A cookbook

LIKES: Cheese

DISLIKES: Diets

FAVORITE VACATION SPOT:
Provence, France

MOST LIKELY TO: Make quiche

DACHSHUND

EYE COLOR: Sky blue

BODY COLOR: Black and brown

FAVORITE ACCESSORY: Pink sweater

LIKES: Getting dressed up

DISLIKES: Closing time

FAVORITE VACATION SPOT: The mall

MOST LIKELY TO: Go shopping

HORSE

EYE COLOR: Grass green

BODY COLOR: White and brown

FAVORITE ACCESSORY: Cowboy hat

LIKES: The rodeo

DISLIKES: Standing still

FAVORITE VACATION SPOT: Glacier National Park, Montana

MOST LIKELY TO: Gallop

HORSE

EYE COLOR: Light blue

BODY COLOR: Brown and white

FAVORITE ACCESSORY: First-place ribbon

LIKES: Contests

DISLIKES: Making mistakes

FAVORITE VACATION SPOT: Cheyenne, Wyoming

MOST LIKELY TO: Eat carrots

CAT

EYE COLOR: Grass green

BODY COLOR: Golden

FAVORITE ACCESSORY: Hairbrush

LIKES: Winning trophies

DISLIKES: Bad hair days

FAVORITE VACATION SPOT: The groomer

MOST LIKELY TO: Pose for a picture

PANDA

EYE COLOR: Grass green

BODY COLOR: Purple and white

FAVORITE ACCESSORY: Bamboo

LIKES: Climbing mountains

DISLIKES: Pollution

FAVORITE VACATION SPOT:
Beijing, China

MOST LIKELY TO: Take a nap

OWL

EYE COLOR: Lavender

BODY COLOR: Reddish brown

FAVORITE ACCESSORY: Glasses

LIKES: Reading novels

DISLIKES: Talking in the library

FAVORITE VACATION SPOT:
Antique bookstores

MOST LIKELY TO:
Stay up late reading

BUTTERFLY

EYE COLOR: Turquoise

BODY COLOR: Turquoise with purple wings

FAVORITE ACCESSORY: Shovel

LIKES: Gardening

DISLIKES: Winter

FAVORITE VACATION SPOT:
A meadow

MOST LIKELY TO:
Stop and smell the roses

TOTALLY TALENTED

These brilliant pets can do it all! Do you and your pets share any talents? If so, this could be the beginning of a beautiful friendship.

GREYHOUND

EYE COLOR: Light blue
BODY COLOR: Gray
FAVORITE ACCESSORY: Stationery
LIKES: Writing stories
DISLIKES: Lost mail
FAVORITE VACATION SPOT:
Florence, Italy
MOST LIKELY TO:
Send you a letter

BUNNY

EYE COLOR: Olive green
BODY COLOR:
Golden and white
FAVORITE ACCESSORY:
MP3 player
LIKES: Making music
DISLIKES: Waking up
FAVORITE VACATION SPOT:
A dance club
MOST LIKELY TO: Stay up late

CAT

EYE COLOR: Mint green

BODY COLOR: White and gray

FAVORITE ACCESSORY: Pom-pom

LIKES: Cheering

DISLIKES: Booing

FAVORITE VACATION SPOT: Cheer camp

MOST LIKELY TO: Shout "Go, team!"

PIG

EYE COLOR: Blue-green

BODY COLOR: Pink

FAVORITE ACCESSORY: Journal

LIKES: Writing poems

DISLIKES: When words don't rhyme

FAVORITE VACATION SPOT: San Francisco, California

MOST LIKELY TO: Write you a poem

CHINCHILLA

EYE COLOR: Light brown

BODY COLOR:
Golden brown and cream

FAVORITE ACCESSORY:
Knit hat

LIKES: Hiking through snow

DISLIKES: When campfires go out

FAVORITE VACATION SPOT:
The Andes Mountains

MOST LIKELY TO: Have the softest fur

HUSKY

EYE COLOR: Ice blue

BODY COLOR:
Brown and white

FAVORITE ACCESSORY:
Snow boots

LIKES: Hanging out in groups

DISLIKES: Being alone

FAVORITE VACATION SPOT:
Juneau, Alaska

MOST LIKELY TO: Play winter sports

SEAL

EYE COLOR: Mint green

BODY COLOR: Gray and white

FAVORITE ACCESSORY: Snorkel

LIKES: Catching fish

DISLIKES: Sharks

FAVORITE VACATION SPOT:
Antarctica

MOST LIKELY TO:
Dive in the water first

LIZARD

EYE COLOR: Purple

BODY COLOR: Blue and green

FAVORITE ACCESSORY:
Activity books

LIKES: Solving puzzles

DISLIKES: Easy games

FAVORITE VACATION SPOT:
The bookstore

MOST LIKELY TO: Play su doku

BIRD

EYE COLOR: Sky blue

BODY COLOR: Pink and yellow

FAVORITE ACCESSORY:
Sheet music

LIKES: Singing

DISLIKES: Being off-key

FAVORITE VACATION SPOT:
The opera house

MOST LIKELY TO:
Be found on stage

IGUANA

EYE COLOR: Lavender

BODY COLOR:
Yellow and green

FAVORITE ACCESSORY:
Sun visor

LIKES: Swimming laps

DISLIKES: Big waves

FAVORITE VACATION SPOT: Fiji

MOST LIKELY TO: Say "Let's take a dip!"

PLAYGROUND PALS

These pets sure know how to play around. They make time for fun and games— and superspecial friends like you!

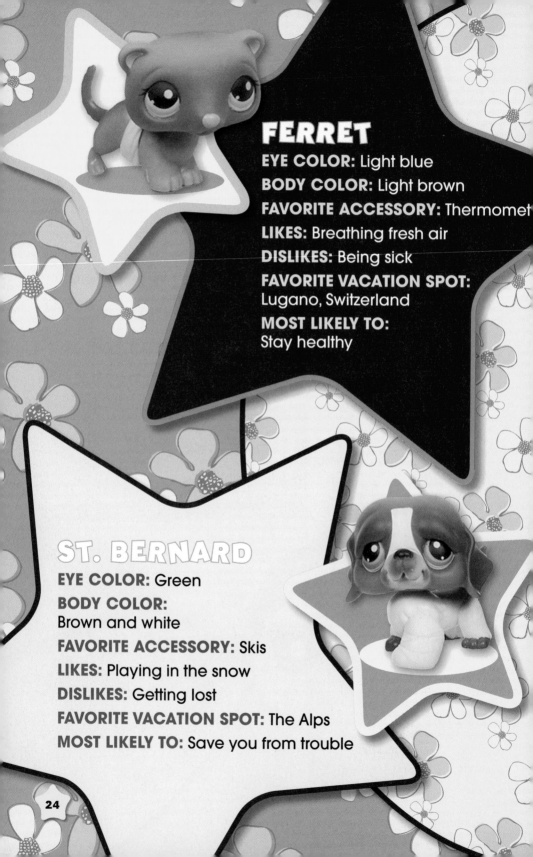

FERRET

EYE COLOR: Light blue

BODY COLOR: Light brown

FAVORITE ACCESSORY: Thermomet

LIKES: Breathing fresh air

DISLIKES: Being sick

FAVORITE VACATION SPOT:
Lugano, Switzerland

MOST LIKELY TO:
Stay healthy

ST. BERNARD

EYE COLOR: Green

BODY COLOR:
Brown and white

FAVORITE ACCESSORY: Skis

LIKES: Playing in the snow

DISLIKES: Getting lost

FAVORITE VACATION SPOT: The Alps

MOST LIKELY TO: Save you from trouble

CAT

EYE COLOR: Sea green

BODY COLOR: Charcoal gray

FAVORITE ACCESSORY:
X-ray machine

LIKES: Looking at bones

DISLIKES: Falling

FAVORITE VACATION SPOT:
Las Vegas, Nevada

MOST LIKELY TO:
Balance on one paw

BIRD

EYE COLOR: Sky blue

BODY COLOR: Gray and white

FAVORITE ACCESSORY:
Post office box

LIKES: Bringing messages

DISLIKES: Fighting

FAVORITE VACATION SPOT:
Rome, Italy

MOST LIKELY TO:
Hand-deliver a package

GERMAN SHEPHERD

EYE COLOR: Dark green

BODY COLOR: Golden and brown

FAVORITE ACCESSORY: Walkie-talkie

LIKES: Chasing criminals

DISLIKES: Standing still

FAVORITE VACATION SPOT: Alcatraz

MOST LIKELY TO: Fight crime

HUSKY

EYE COLOR: Yellow-green

BODY COLOR: Gray and white

FAVORITE ACCESSORY: Sneakers

LIKES: Working out

DISLIKES: Being lazy

FAVORITE VACATION SPOT: The gym

MOST LIKELY TO: Go for a run

CHIMP

EYE COLOR: Lavender

BODY COLOR: Brown and tan

FAVORITE ACCESSORY:
Bongo drums

LIKES: Living in the trees

DISLIKES: The cold

FAVORITE VACATION SPOT:
Cairo, Egypt

MOST LIKELY TO:
Start a drum circle

BIRD

EYE COLOR: Sky blue

BODY COLOR: Pink and blue

FAVORITE ACCESSORY: Hair spray

LIKES: Having a Mohawk

DISLIKES: Soft music

FAVORITE VACATION SPOT:
London, England

MOST LIKELY TO:
Go to a punk concert

MONKEY

EYE COLOR: Grass green

BODY COLOR: Golden and cream

FAVORITE ACCESSORY: Trapeze

LIKES: Being upside down

DISLIKES: Unripe bananas

FAVORITE VACATION SPOT: Amazon rain forest

MOST LIKELY TO: Do a backflip

CAT

EYE COLOR: Emerald green

BODY COLOR: Golden and cream

FAVORITE ACCESSORY: Wool scarf

LIKES: Making snow angels

DISLIKES: Cold paws

FAVORITE VACATION SPOT: Nova Scotia, Canada

MOST LIKELY TO: Wear a sweater

SUPER SASSY

These little pets
have tons of spunk.
Do you think you
have the energy
to keep up?

COCKER SPANIEL

EYE COLOR: Light green

BODY COLOR: Golden and cream

FAVORITE ACCESSORY: Shopping cart

LIKES: New clothes

DISLIKES: Holes in clothes

FAVORITE VACATION SPOT: Miami, Florida

MOST LIKELY TO: Max out a credit card

BIRD

EYE COLOR: Grass green

BODY COLOR: Pink and green

FAVORITE ACCESSORY: Pointy beak

LIKES: Feeding on nectar

DISLIKES: Flowers that don't smell sweet

FAVORITE VACATION SPOT: A garden

MOST LIKELY TO: Flap around

CAT

EYE COLOR: Pale blue

BODY COLOR: Gray and white

FAVORITE ACCESSORY:
Fishing rod

LIKES: Fish

DISLIKES: Thunderstorms

FAVORITE VACATION SPOT:
On a fishing boat

MOST LIKELY TO: Reel one in

BUNNY

EYE COLOR: Blue

BODY COLOR: Gray and white

FAVORITE ACCESSORY:
Watering can

LIKES: Fresh veggies

DISLIKES: Canned food

FAVORITE VACATION SPOT:
Twin Falls, Idaho

MOST LIKELY TO:
Plant a vegetable patch

DOG

EYE COLOR: Green

BODY COLOR: Cream and golden

FAVORITE ACCESSORY: Stethosco

LIKES: Listening to your heart

DISLIKES: Germs

FAVORITE VACATION SPOT: Tucson, Arizona

MOST LIKELY TO: Take vitamins

CAT

EYE COLOR: Blue

BODY COLOR: Golden and white

FAVORITE ACCESSORY: Toothbrush

LIKES: Candy

DISLIKES: Cavities

FAVORITE VACATION SPOT: Candy shop

MOST LIKELY TO: Get a stomachache

MONKEY

EYE COLOR: Dark blue

BODY COLOR: Brown and tan

FAVORITE ACCESSORY: Weights

LIKES: Staying in shape

DISLIKES: Sore muscles

FAVORITE VACATION SPOT:
The basketball court

MOST LIKELY TO:
Make a jump shot

AQUARIUM FRIENDS

Dive in! The water's just right! These little critters are waiting for someone special— just like you—to splash around with.

TURTLE

EYE COLOR: Purple

BODY COLOR: Green and brown

FAVORITE ACCESSORY: Surfboard

LIKES: Catching waves

DISLIKES: Calm waters

FAVORITE VACATION SPOT: Melbourne, Australia

MOST LIKELY TO: Hang ten

SEA HORSE

EYE COLOR: Lavender

BODY COLOR: Light green, yellow, and pink

FAVORITE ACCESSORY: Bubble bath

LIKES: Long baths

DISLIKES: Cold water

FAVORITE VACATION SPOT: Costa Rica

MOST LIKELY TO: Float

HERMIT CRAB

EYE COLOR: Seaweed green

BODY COLOR: Orange and purple

FAVORITE ACCESSORY: Flip-flops

LIKES: Looking for new shells

DISLIKES: Outgrowing old shells

FAVORITE VACATION SPOT:
Malibu, California

MOST LIKELY TO:
Take a stroll on the beach

DOG DAYS

These doggies are looking for a friend just like you. They're loyal, friendly, and most of all, cuddly. So get outside and have some fun with these little pups!

CORGIE

EYE COLOR: Green

BODY COLOR: Gray

FAVORITE ACCESSORY: Dog bone

LIKES: Working hard

DISLIKES: Lying around

FAVORITE VACATION SPOT:
Cardiff, Wales

MOST LIKELY TO:
Invite friends over

DOG

EYE COLOR: Slate blue

BODY COLOR: Golden brown

FAVORITE ACCESSORY: Baby doll

LIKES: Being tucked in

DISLIKES: Scary bedtime stories

FAVORITE VACATION SPOT:
An amusement park

MOST LIKELY TO: Give you a hug

FANCIEST PETS

Whether these animals are traveling the world, looking at art, or getting dressed up, they are far fancier than all the rest.

BUNNY

EYE COLOR: Turquoise

BODY COLOR: White, black, pink

FAVORITE ACCESSORY: Cookbook

LIKES: Baking

DISLIKES: Soufflés that don't rise

FAVORITE VACATION SPOT:
The South of France

MOST LIKELY TO:
Invent a new recipe

GECKO

EYE COLOR: Yellow-green

BODY COLOR: Mint green

FAVORITE ACCESSORY: Flashlight

LIKES: Exploring caves

DISLIKES: Running

FAVORITE VACATION SPOT:
The Galápagos Islands

MOST LIKELY TO:
Go on adventures

DOG

EYE COLOR: Blue and brown

BODY COLOR: Light and dark gray

FAVORITE ACCESSORY: Opera glasses

LIKES: Watching opera

DISLIKES: Having bad seats

FAVORITE VACATION SPOT:
Sydney, Australia

MOST LIKELY TO: Shout "Bravo!"

CAT

EYE COLOR:
Yellow and orange

BODY COLOR:
Orange and white

FAVORITE ACCESSORY:
Art history book

LIKES: Modern art

DISLIKES: Abstract art

FAVORITE VACATION SPOT:
Paris, France

MOST LIKELY TO:
Carry a sketchbook

BIRD

EYE COLOR: Turquoise

BODY COLOR:
Pink and yellow

FAVORITE ACCESSORY:
Microphone

LIKES: Being on stage

DISLIKES: Forgetting lyrics

FAVORITE VACATION SPOT:
Los Angeles, California

MOST LIKELY TO: Start a band

BIRD

EYE COLOR: Light green

BODY COLOR: Lavender

FAVORITE ACCESSORY: Twigs

LIKES: Architecture

DISLIKES: Rain

FAVORITE VACATION SPOT:
In the treetops

MOST LIKELY TO:
Build a nest

PEACOCK

EYE COLOR: Green

BODY COLOR: Blue and green

FAVORITE ACCESSORY:
Its feathers

LIKES: Showing off

DISLIKES: Being plain

FAVORITE VACATION SPOT:
Mumbai, India

MOST LIKELY TO: Strut

RAT

EYE COLOR: Gray-blue

BODY COLOR: Golden brown

FAVORITE ACCESSORY: Crackers

LIKES: Appetizers

DISLIKES: Missing meals

FAVORITE VACATION SPOT: A chef's kitchen

MOST LIKELY TO: Crawl in tight spaces

CAT

EYE COLOR Moss green

BODY COLOR: White and pink

FAVORITE ACCESSORY: Black eyeliner

LIKES: Fashion shows

DISLIKES: Last season's clothes

FAVORITE VACATION SPOT: Milan, Italy

MOST LIKELY TO: Hire a stylist

BUNNY

EYE COLOR: Teal

BODY COLOR: Yellow and purple

FAVORITE ACCESSORY: Tissues

LIKES: Laughing

DISLIKES: Unhappy endings

FAVORITE VACATION SPOT:
Hollywood, California

MOST LIKELY TO:
Cry at sad movies

BIRD

EYE COLOR: Light blue

BODY COLOR:
Light green, blue, and orange

FAVORITE ACCESSORY: Compass

LIKES: Airplanes

DISLIKES: Bad weather

FAVORITE VACATION SPOT: The sky

MOST LIKELY TO: Be a pilot

CAT

EYE COLOR: Blue

BODY COLOR:
Cream and brown

FAVORITE ACCESSORY:
Italy guidebook

LIKES: Learning Italian

DISLIKES: Confusing maps

FAVORITE VACATION SPOT:
Venice, Italy

MOST LIKELY TO: Order pizza

TURTLE

EYE COLOR: Purple and blue

BODY COLOR:
Blue, green, brown

FAVORITE ACCESSORY:
Skateboard

LIKES: Fast music

DISLIKES: Slow music

FAVORITE VACATION SPOT:
San Diego, California

MOST LIKELY TO: Download music

FERRET

EYE COLOR: Blue

BODY COLOR: White and pink

FAVORITE ACCESSORY: Dominoes

LIKES: Relaxing

DISLIKES: Heavy metal music

FAVORITE VACATION SPOT: Miami, Florida

MOST LIKELY TO: Say "I'm sleepy."

CAT

EYE COLOR: Olive green

BODY COLOR: Orange, white, and pink

FAVORITE ACCESSORY: Earmuffs

LIKES: Zooming

DISLIKES: Slush

FAVORITE VACATION SPOT: Aspen, Colorado

MOST LIKELY TO: Go snowboarding

BIRD

EYE COLOR: Sky blue

BODY COLOR: Light yellow

FAVORITE ACCESSORY: Sunglasses

LIKES: Traveling south

DISLIKES: Going to bed early

FAVORITE VACATION SPOT: Maui, Hawaii

MOST LIKELY TO: Hula dance

DOG

EYE COLOR: Ice blue

BODY COLOR: Brown, white, pink

FAVORITE ACCESSORY: Chopsticks

LIKES: Noodles

DISLIKES: Seasickness

FAVORITE VACATION SPOT: Seoul, Korea

MOST LIKELY TO: Sing karaoke

DRAGONFLY

EYE COLOR: Sky blue

BODY COLOR: Pink

FAVORITE ACCESSORY:
Its wings

LIKES: The summer

DISLIKES: The rain

FAVORITE VACATION SPOT:
The countryside

MOST LIKELY TO:
Soar through the air

BIRD

EYE COLOR: Grass green

BODY COLOR:
Lavender, purple, and white

FAVORITE ACCESSORY: Paint

LIKES: Art

DISLIKES: Loud people

FAVORITE VACATION SPOT:
Tuscany, Italy

MOST LIKELY TO:
Sleep at the movies

TURTLE

EYE COLOR: Green

BODY COLOR: Light green and pink

FAVORITE ACCESSORY: Shell

LIKES: Being slow

DISLIKES: Fast food

FAVORITE VACATION SPOT:
Myrtle Beach, South Carolina

MOST LIKELY TO:
Never break the speed limit

BUNNY

EYE COLOR: Green

BODY COLOR: Yellow and pink

FAVORITE ACCESSORY: Jump rope

LIKES: Playing games

DISLIKES: Sitting still

FAVORITE VACATION SPOT:
Dallas, Texas

MOST LIKELY TO: Go to the circus

GROOVIEST PETS

These groovy pets
like chilling out and
spending time with
their favorite friends.
So sit back, relax, and
enjoy the ride.

DEER

EYE COLOR: Fuchsia

BODY COLOR: Orange and yellow

FAVORITE ACCESSORY:
Flower face paint

LIKES: Peace

DISLIKES: War

FAVORITE VACATION SPOT:
Woodstock, New York

MOST LIKELY TO: Dance

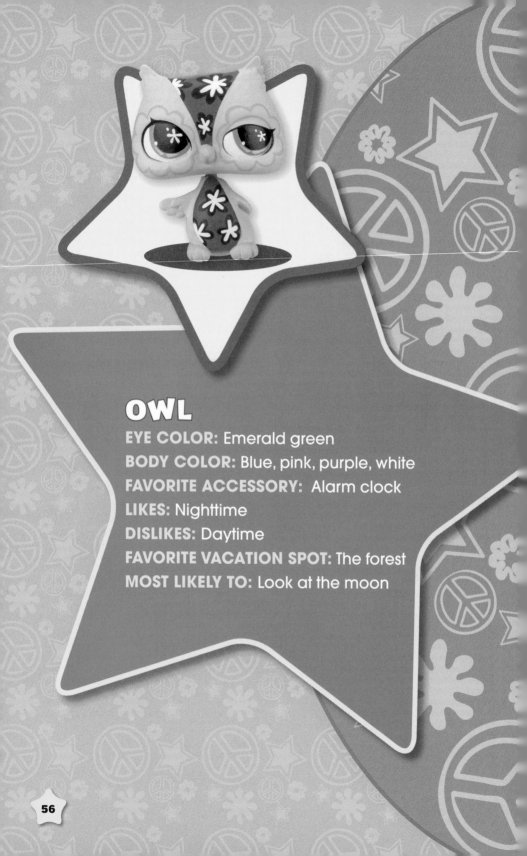

OWL

EYE COLOR: Emerald green

BODY COLOR: Blue, pink, purple, white

FAVORITE ACCESSORY: Alarm clock

LIKES: Nighttime

DISLIKES: Daytime

FAVORITE VACATION SPOT: The forest

MOST LIKELY TO: Look at the moon

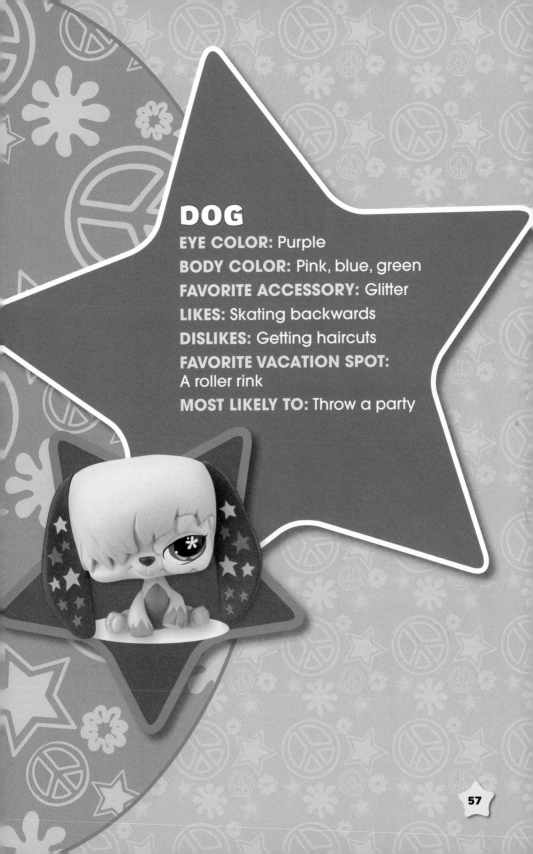

DOG

EYE COLOR: Purple

BODY COLOR: Pink, blue, green

FAVORITE ACCESSORY: Glitter

LIKES: Skating backwards

DISLIKES: Getting haircuts

FAVORITE VACATION SPOT:
A roller rink

MOST LIKELY TO: Throw a party

PUNKIEST PETS

Turn up the volume
and get ready to
party! These pets
are totally punk
and ready to rock
out with you!

BAT

EYE COLOR: Light blue

BODY COLOR: Purple, pink, light green

FAVORITE ACCESSORY: Skull bow

LIKES: Horror movies

DISLIKES: Happy endings

FAVORITE VACATION SPOT: A cave

MOST LIKELY TO: Stay out late

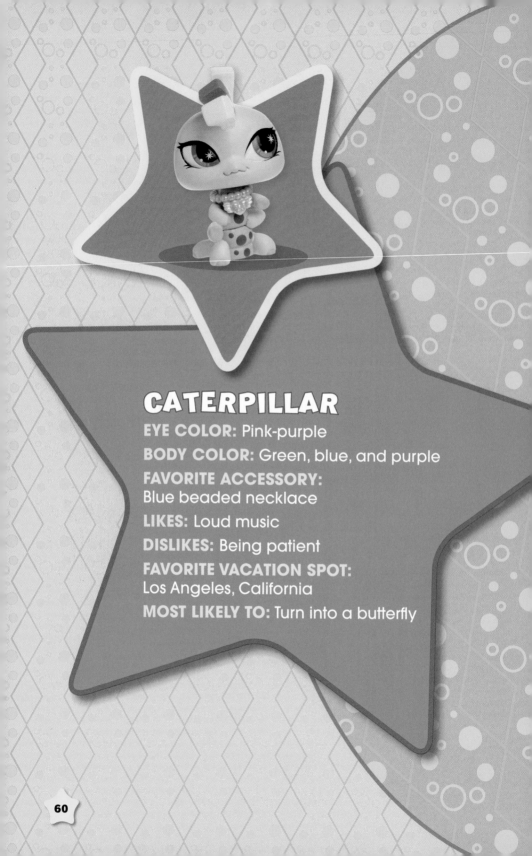

CATERPILLAR

EYE COLOR: Pink-purple

BODY COLOR: Green, blue, and purple

FAVORITE ACCESSORY:
Blue beaded necklace

LIKES: Loud music

DISLIKES: Being patient

FAVORITE VACATION SPOT:
Los Angeles, California

MOST LIKELY TO: Turn into a butterfly

IGUANA

EYE COLOR: Blue

BODY COLOR: Light green, purple, pink

FAVORITE ACCESSORY: Heart necklace

LIKES: Dressing up

DISLIKES: Country music

FAVORITE VACATION SPOT:
New York, New York

MOST LIKELY TO: Be in a band

HOW BIG IS YOUR LITTLEST PET SHOP?
CHECK 'EM OUT!

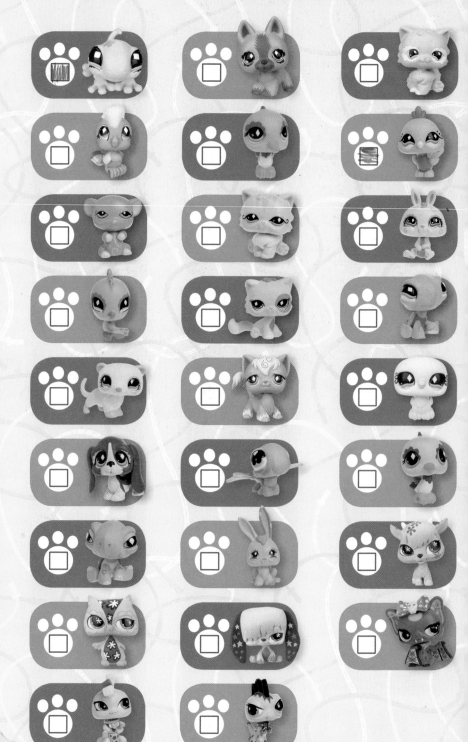